Contents

Science Units

My Skeletal System

Big Question: Can I live without my bones?

Earth's Moon and Sun

Big Question: Would you like to visit the moon or the sun?

Everything Is Made of Matter

Big Question: What is the same about water, a toy, and air?

Animal Classification

Big Question: Why do animals have different kinds of teeth?

Social Studies Units

American Songs and Symbols

Big Question: What songs and symbols tell me I'm in America?

Art Has Meaning

Big Question: What do you think when you look at art?

People Find Solutions

Big Question: How can a great idea make our lives better?

EMC 6421

Evan-Moor®
Helping Children Learn

Reorder No. (5-Pack)
EMC 6431

Correlated to State and Common Core State Standards

Congratulations on your purchase of some of the finest teaching materials in the world.

No part of this book may be reproduced in any form or stored in any retrieval system without the written permission of publisher.

For information about other Evan-Moor products, call 1-800-777-4362, fax 1-800-777-4332, or visit our Web site, www.evan-moor.com.
Entire contents © 2014 EVAN-MOOR CORP.
18 Lower Ragsdale Drive, Monterey, CA 93940-5746. Printed in USA.

CPSIA: Printed by McNaughton & Gunn, Saline, MI USA. [1/2014]

Jacob's Arm

Name: _____

Boom, crash, ouch!
Jacob fell off his bike.
His arm hurt a lot!

1

Dr. Beck looked at an X-ray of Jacob's arm.
His arm bone was broken.

2

Dr. Beck put a cast on Jacob's arm.
He told Jacob how to take care of himself.

3

Jacob ate healthy food.
He drank a lot of water.

4

Jacob went for a walk every day.
He got a lot of rest, too.

5

Jacob wanted to ride his bike.
It looked like fun.

6

Six weeks went by.
Jacob's arm was better.
Then he could ride his bike again.

7

Dictionary

Read each word aloud.

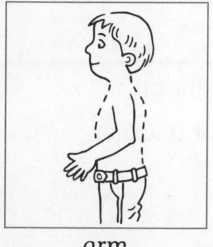

arm

bike

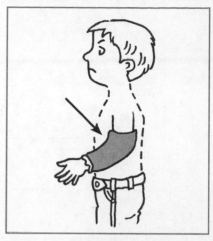

cast

drank

healthy food

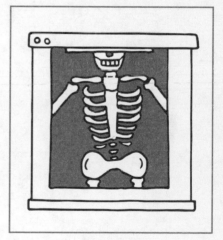

X-ray

Words to Know

bone	boom	broken	crash
himself	hurt	ouch	rest
ride	water	weeks	

I Read Closely

Look at the picture. Read the sentences.
Mark the sentence that goes with the picture.

1

○ Jacob fell off his bike.

○ Jacob went for a walk.

2

○ Jacob's mom put a cast on his arm.

○ Dr. Beck put a cast on Jacob's arm.

3

○ Jacob ate healthy food.

○ Jacob got a lot of rest.

4

○ It took ten weeks for Jacob's arm to get better.

○ It took six weeks for Jacob's arm to get better.

I Use New Words

Write the missing word to complete the sentence.
Then read the sentence.

1   X-ray   ouch

An _____ can show a broken bone.

2   rest   ride

You can _____ a bike.

3   weeks   water

We drank _____.

4   healthy   broken

I feel good when I eat _____ food.

5   crash   arm

I have a cast on my _____.

I Write About It

1 Draw a picture to show what Jacob did to help his arm get better.

2 Write about your picture.

_____

_____

_____

_____

_____

_____

How Bones Work

Name: _____

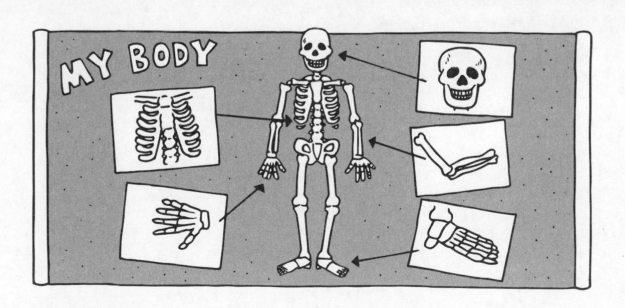

You have more than 200 bones.
Bones make up your skeleton.

1

Bones are alive.
They grow and change.

2

Bones give you shape.
They help you run, jump, and sit.

3

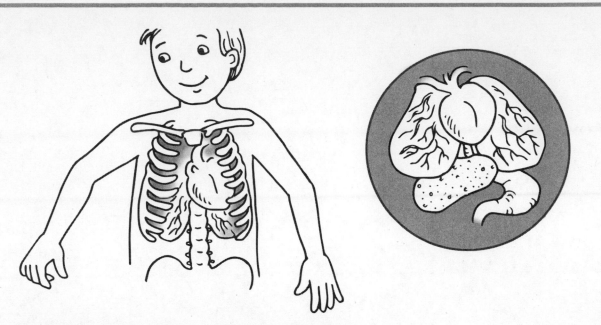

Bones do other things, too.
Some bones keep body parts safe.

4

Bone Parts

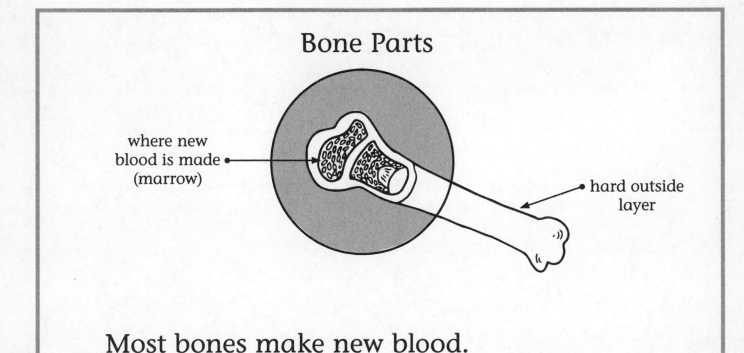

where new
blood is made
(marrow)

hard outside
layer

Most bones make new blood.
Blood is made inside a bone.

5

Bones meet at a joint.
A joint lets you bend and move.

6

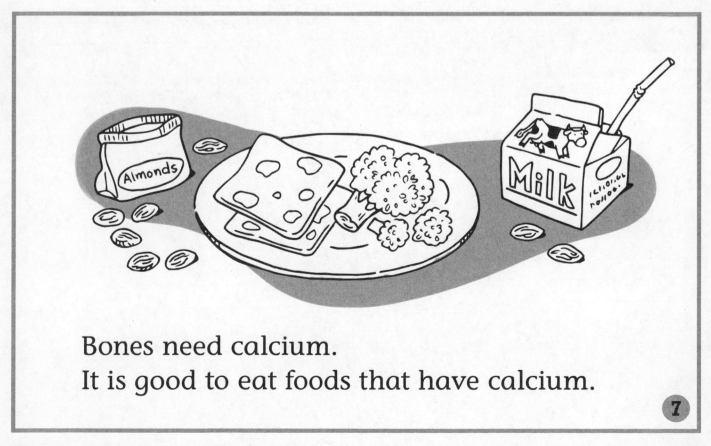

Bones need calcium.
It is good to eat foods that have calcium.

7

Dictionary

Read each word aloud.

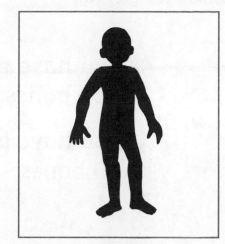

bend

body

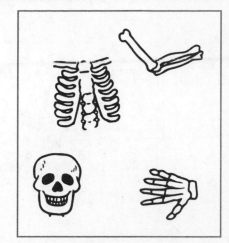

bones

grow

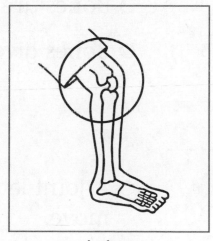

joint

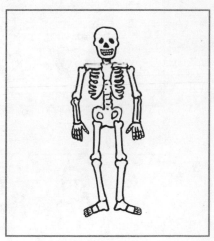

skeleton

Words to Know

alive	blood	calcium	change
foods	inside	move	parts
safe	shape	work	

I Read Closely

Look at the picture. Read the sentences.
Mark the sentence that goes with the picture.

1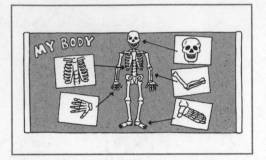

    ○ You have more than 200 bones.

    ○ You have less than 50 bones.

2

    ○ Bones are not alive.

    ○ Bones give you shape.

3

    ○ A joint lets you bend and move.

    ○ A joint keeps you safe.

4

    ○ Bones need calcium.

    ○ Shapes need calcium.

Reading Paired Text • EMC 6421 • © Evan-Moor Corp.

I Use New Words

Write the missing word to complete the sentence.
Then read the sentence.

1   safe   calcium

Some foods have _____.

2   bone   joint

A _____ lets you bend.

3   skeleton   change

A _____ is made of bones.

4   foods   parts

Bones and joints are body _____.

5   alive   work

Bones are _____.

I Write About It

1 Draw a picture of how you would look if you did <u>not</u> have a skeleton.
Hint: Could you sit on a bike seat?

2 Could you ride a bike with no bones in your body? Write about it.

_____

_____

_____

3 Write a sentence to tell how you are using your joints now.

_____

_____

_____

I Read and Understand

Read the sentence. Mark the best answer.

1 Your body has bones that make up a ____.

- ○ cast
- ○ bike
- ○ skeleton

2 Joints help you ____.

- ○ drink water
- ○ bend and move
- ○ eat food with calcium

3 ____ is good for your bones.

- ○ Healthy food
- ○ A big crash
- ○ A broken bike

4 Bones keep your ____ safe.

- ○ X-ray
- ○ move
- ○ body parts

I Can!

> I can tell you about my skeleton and how I can take care of my bones.

1

Draw a picture of something that helps broken bones get better.	Draw a picture of something that is good for your bones.

2 What are some ways that your bones help you live? Write about them.

_____

_____

_____

_____

_____

_____

Are the Moon and the Sun the Same?

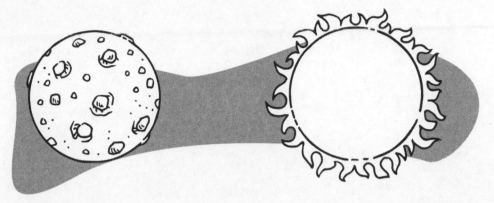

Name: _____

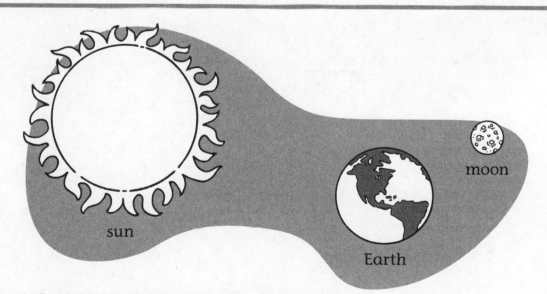

Earth has a moon and a sun.
The moon and sun are both in the sky.
They are both far, far away.

1

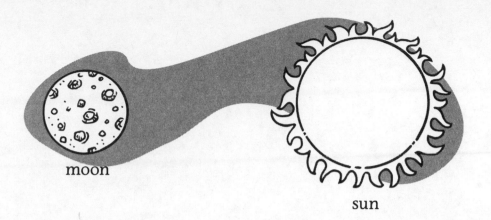

moon

sun

The moon and the sun are not the same.
The moon is made mostly of rock.
The sun is a star made of hot gases.

2

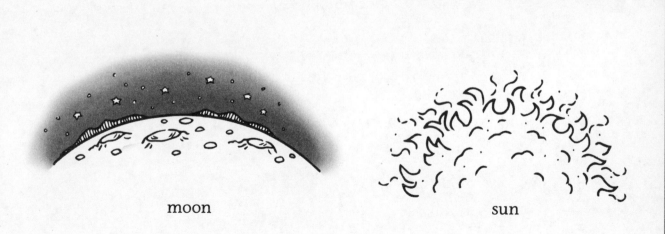

moon

sun

The moon and the sun are not the same.
The moon has a solid surface.
The sun does not have a solid surface.

3

moon

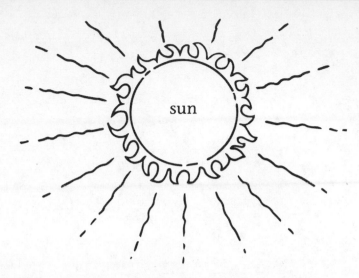

sun

The moon and the sun are not the same.
The moon does not make light and heat.
The sun makes light and heat.

4

The moon and the sun are not the same.
The moon does not shine on the sun.
The sun shines on the moon.

5

The moon and sun are not the same.
People have walked on the moon.
People can't go near the sun.

6

Comparing the Moon and the Sun

	Very Far Away	Made of Rock	Made of Hot Gases	Makes Light	People Have Walked on It
moon	X	X			X
sun	X		X	X	

Now I know that the moon and the sun are not the same!

7

Dictionary

Read each word aloud.

Earth

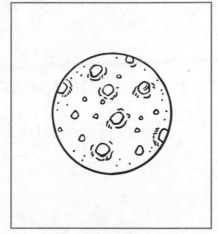

moon

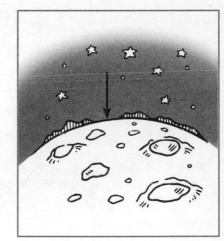

rock

sky

sun

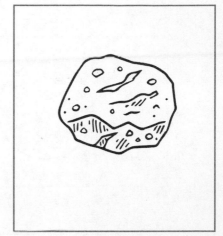

surface

Words to Know

far	gases	heat	light
mostly	near	people	same
shine	solid	star	walked

I Read Closely

Look at the picture. Read the sentences.
Mark the sentence that goes with the picture.

 1

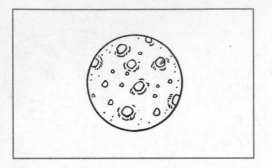

○ The moon is mostly rock.

○ The sun is mostly rock.

 2

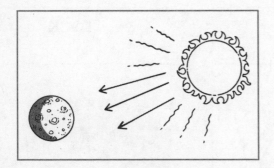

○ The sun shines on the moon.

○ The moon shines on the sun.

 3

○ The moon is a star made of hot gases.

○ The sun is a star made of hot gases.

 4

○ People can't go near the sun.

○ People have walked on the sun.

Reading Paired Text • EMC 6421 • © Evan-Moor Corp.

I Use New Words

Write the missing word to complete the sentence.
Then read the sentence.

1   rock   star

The sun is a _____.

2   same   gases

The moon and sun are not the _____.

3   sky   heat

I see the moon in the _____.

4   rock   sun

The _____ shines.

5   light   Earth

People can walk on _____.

I Write About It

1 Write a sentence that tells how the moon and the sun are not the same.

_____

_____

_____

2 Would you like to walk on the moon or the sun? Write about it.

_____

_____

_____

_____

_____

Draw a picture about what you wrote.

Earth's Moon

Name: _____

We can see the moon in space.
It is smaller than Earth.

The moon has no air.
No people, plants, or animals live there.

2

People have walked on the moon.
They wore special suits.
They took air to breathe.

3

Many space rocks hit the moon.
The rocks make big craters.

4

The sun shines its light on the moon.
We see the part of the moon that the
sun shines on.

5

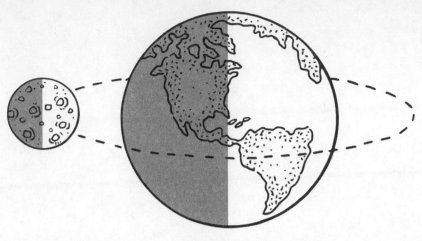

moon's orbit

The moon moves around Earth
every 29 days. The part of the moon
that we can see changes.

6

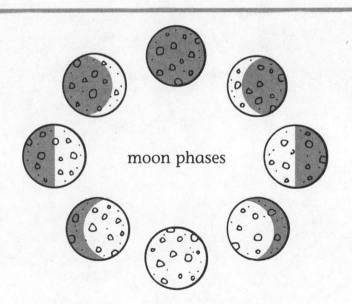

moon phases

The moon looks like it changes shape.
It looks different every night.

7

Dictionary

Read each word aloud.

air

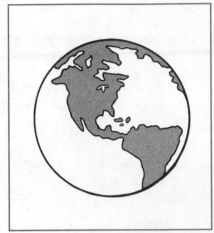

craters

Earth

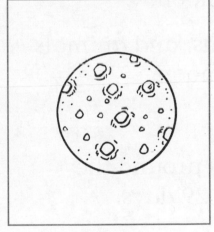

moon

space

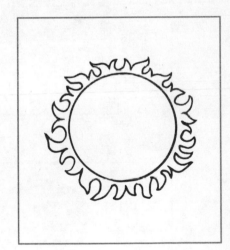

sun

Words to Know

breathe	changes	different	light
live	night	part	shines
smaller	special	suits	wore

I Read Closely

Look at the picture. Read the sentences.
Mark the sentence that goes with the picture.

1

○ We cannot see the moon in space.

○ We can see the moon in space.

2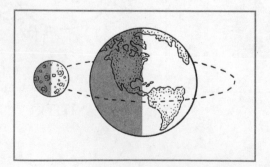

○ No people, plants, or animals live on the moon.

○ People, plants, and animals live on the moon.

3

○ Earth moves around the moon every 29 days.

○ The moon moves around Earth every 29 days.

4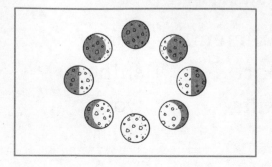

○ The moon changes shape.

○ The moon looks like it changes shape.

Reading Paired Text • EMC 6421 • © Evan-Moor Corp.

I Use New Words

Write the missing word to complete the sentence.
Then read the sentence.

1   light   crater

A big rock makes a _____ on the moon.

2   Earth   space

We live on _____.

3   shines   suits

The sun _____ on the moon.

4   air   animals

We need _____ to breathe.

5   wore   changes

The moon looks like it _____ shape.

I Write About It

Look at the picture. Answer the questions.

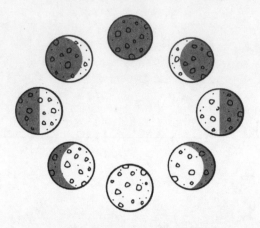

1 Does the moon really change shape?
Write a sentence to tell about it.

_____

_____

_____

_____

_____

2 How does the moon get craters?
Write a sentence to tell about it.

_____

_____

_____

_____

I Read and Understand

Read the sentence. Mark the best answer.

1 The moon is made mostly of _____.

   ○ rock

   ○ plants

   ○ gases

2 The _____ makes light and heat.

   ○ Earth

   ○ sun

   ○ moon

3 The sun does not have a solid _____.

   ○ crater

   ○ air

   ○ surface

4 People have walked on the _____.

   ○ star

   ○ moon

   ○ sun

I Can!

I can share facts about the moon and the sun.

1 Write three facts about the moon and the sun.

moon	sun
1. _____	1. _____
2. _____	2. _____
3. _____	3. _____

2 Would you like to visit the moon or the sun? Write about it.

_____

_____

_____

_____

_____

_____

_____

What Is Matter?

Name: _____

Everything around us is made of matter.
Matter can be solid, liquid, or gas.

1

Matter can be a solid.
A solid has a shape of its own.
A book is a solid. A toy is a solid.

2

Matter can be a liquid.
A liquid has no shape of its own.
Water is a liquid. Juice is a liquid.

3

Matter can be a gas.
A gas has no shape of its own.
Air is a gas. Steam is a gas.

solid   liquid   gas

A solid keeps its shape.
A liquid can flow.
A gas can float.

5

All of these things are matter.

6

Everything is made of matter.
Matter is all around us.

7

Dictionary

Read each word aloud.

air

float

flow

gas

liquid

solid

Words to Know

everything	juice	matter	own
shape	steam	toy	water

I Read Closely

Look at the picture. Read the sentences.
Mark the sentence that goes with the picture.

1

○ A solid has a shape.

○ A liquid has a shape.

2

○ Air is a gas.

○ Juice is a gas.

3

○ A solid can flow.

○ A liquid can flow.

4

○ Everything is made of matter.

○ Everything is a solid.

I Use New Words

Write the missing word to complete the sentence.
Then read the sentence.

1   air   toys

My _____ are solids.

2   flow   solid

Water can _____.

3   water   matter

Everything is made of _____.

4   solid   shape

Juice has no _____.

5   liquid   gas

Air is a _____.

I Write About It

1 Look at the picture. Write **S** on something that is a solid. Write **L** on something that is a liquid. Then write **G** on something that is a gas.

2 Look around you. Write a sentence about something you see for each form of matter.

solid

_____

_____

liquid

_____

_____

gas

_____

_____

Wonderful Water

Name: _____

Think about water.
Is it solid, liquid, or gas?

1

It can be all three!
Water is wonderful!

2

Water can be a liquid.
Water can flow, splash, and drip.

3

Water can be a gas.
The gas is called steam.
Steam floats.

4

Water can be a solid.
When water freezes, it turns into a solid.
Solid water is ice.

5

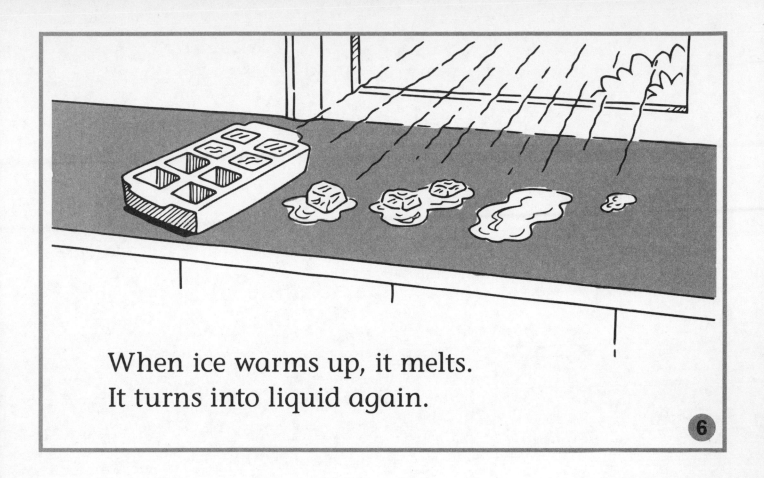

When ice warms up, it melts.
It turns into liquid again.

6

Water is wonderful.
It can be solid, liquid, or gas.

7

Dictionary

Read each word aloud.

drip

floats

flow

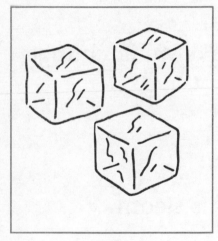

ice

melts

splash

Words to Know

freezes	gas	liquid	solid
steam	think	turns	warms
water	wonderful		

I Read Closely

Look at the picture. Read the sentences.
Mark the sentence that goes with the picture.

1

○ Solid water is gas.

○ Solid water is ice.

2

○ Heat will make ice melt to a liquid.

○ Heat will make water change to a solid.

3

○ Liquid water is steam.

○ Liquid water can flow.

4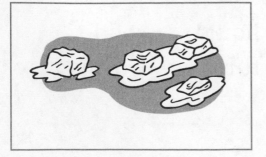

○ If ice warms up, it melts.

○ If ice warms up, it freezes.

I Use New Words

Write the missing word to complete the sentence.
Then read the sentence.

1

> glass   think

I can put water in a _____.

2

> heat   gas

Steam is a _____.

3

> solid   liquid

Water that freezes turns into a _____.

4

> freeze   flow

If you spill water, it will _____.

5

> melt   splash

Ice will _____ in the sun.

I Write About It

1　Draw pictures of water as solid, liquid, and gas. Label each picture.

2　How can you make water change from a solid to a liquid? Write about it.

_____

_____

_____

3　How can you make water change from a liquid to a gas? Write about it.

_____

_____

_____

　　　　　　　　Reading Paired Text • EMC 6421 • © Evan-Moor Corp.

I Read and Understand

Read the sentence. Mark the best answer.

1 The forms of matter are ____.

   ○ solid, big, liquid

   ○ solid, liquid, gas

   ○ liquid, gas, hot

2 Ice, toys, and books are ____.

   ○ solids

   ○ liquids

   ○ gases

3 Steam is water that changed to a ____.

   ○ gas

   ○ liquid

   ○ matter

4 Everything around us is made of ____.

   ○ gas

   ○ solids

   ○ matter

I Can!

I can tell you about the three forms of matter.

1 Draw something to show each form of matter.

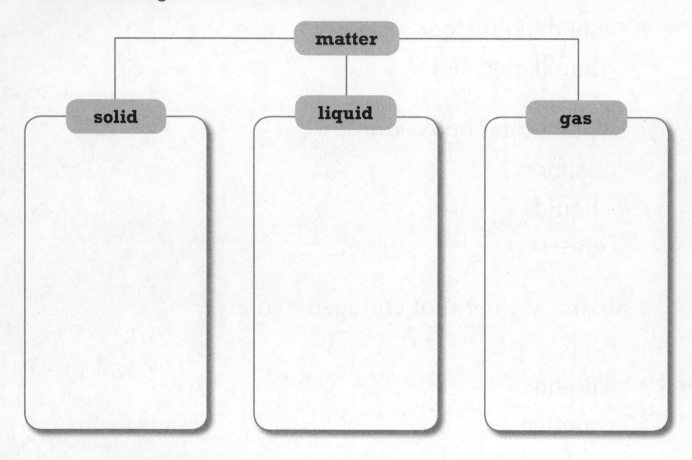

matter

solid   liquid   gas

2 What is the same about water, a toy, and air?
Write a sentence that tells about it.

_____

_____

_____

_____

Goats

Goats are plant eaters,
No meat will do.
Goats want grass to crunch
And plants to chew.

Goats think trees and bark
Are really yummy.
Some roses and grass
Are good for a goat's tummy.

A goat's teeth can grind,
Because they are flat on top.
Goats chew side to side
Until they are ready to stop.

If you need to mow,
I give you this clue.
A small herd of goats
Can mow for you.

Goat Teeth

A baby goat is called a kid.
A kid goat's teeth change as it grows.
A kid goat loses its baby teeth like you do.
Then bigger teeth grow in.
See how a kid goat's teeth change?

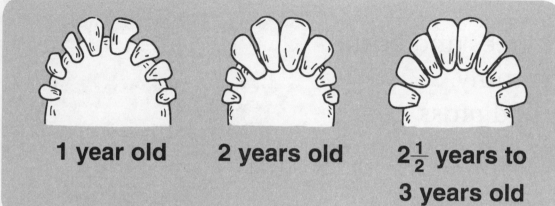

1 year old   **2 years old**   **$2\frac{1}{2}$ years to 3 years old**

The kid goat will grow up.
It will grow teeth that are bigger.
The kid goat will grow teeth that
    are flat on top.
A goat needs to eat plants.
Flat teeth can grind plants.
A goat can eat the food
    that it needs.

Dictionary

Read each word aloud.

chew

goats

herd

mow

roses

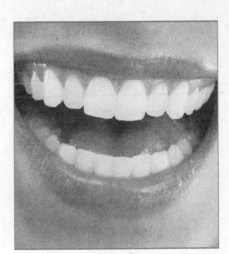

teeth

Words to Know

bark	because	change	clue
crunch	eaters	flat	grind
meat	think	tummy	yummy

I Read Closely

Look at the picture. Read the sentences.
Mark the sentence that goes with the picture.

1

    ○ Goats like to eat meat.

    ○ Goats like to eat plants.

2

    ○ Some roses and grass are good for a goat's tummy.

    ○ Trees and bark are good for a goat's tummy.

3

    ○ Goat teeth are funny.

    ○ Goat teeth are flat.

4

    ○ Goats can help mow.

    ○ Goats can give you a clue.

I Use New Words

Write the missing word to complete the sentence.
Then read the sentence.

1 clue   crunch

A _____ helps you find out.

2 think   mow

To cut the grass is to _____.

3 grind   herd

A lot of goats is a _____.

4 yummy   tummy

A food you like to eat is _____.

5 meat   chew

I _____ my food when I eat.

I Write About It

1 Draw a picture of a food that is good for goats to eat.
Then write about it.

_____

_____

_____

_____

_____

2 What is something that goats can do for you?
Write about it.

_____

_____

_____

_____

_____

Word Bank

crunch   eat   grind   mow   plants

Wild About Food

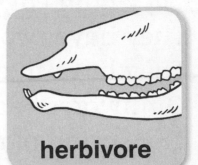

herbivore

How are a rabbit and a deer the same?
They both eat plants.
Animals that eat plants are called
   herbivores.
Herbivores have flat teeth.
They can chew and grind plants.
Plants are good for herbivores.
Herbivores eat all day long.

carnivore

How are a tiger and a wolf the same?
They both eat meat.
Animals that eat other animals are
   called carnivores.
Carnivores have sharp, pointed teeth.
They need to bite meat.
Meat is good for carnivores.
They hunt and eat a lot.

How are a bear and a raccoon the same?
They both eat plants and animals.
They have two kinds of teeth.
They have sharp and flat teeth.
Omnivores bite and chew meat.
They grind plants, too.
Some omnivores eat eggs or bugs.
Plants and animals are good
   for omnivores.

Animals in the wild eat the kind
   of food that is good for them.

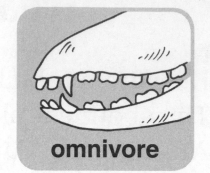

omnivore

Dictionary

Read each word aloud.

bite

chew

eggs

flat

pointed

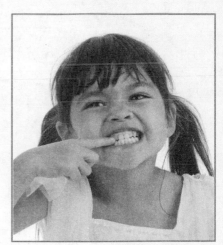

teeth

Words to Know

animals	called	carnivore	grind
herbivore	hunt	long	meat
omnivore	same	sharp	wild

I Read Closely

Look at the picture. Read the sentences.
Mark the sentence that goes with the picture.

1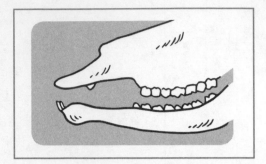

○ A herbivore has flat teeth.

○ A herbivore has sharp teeth.

2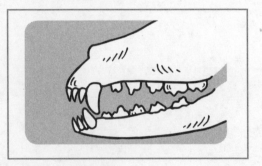

○ A carnivore has flat and sharp teeth.

○ A carnivore has only sharp teeth.

3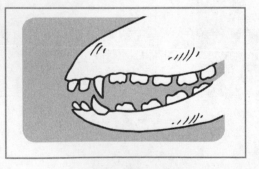

○ An omnivore has only flat teeth.

○ An omnivore has flat and sharp teeth.

4

○ I am an omnivore.

○ I am a herbivore.

I Use New Words

Write the missing word to complete the sentence.
Then read the sentence.

1   teeth   eggs

The bird sat on three _____.

2   Herbivores   Carnivores

_____ eat plants.

3   hunt   flat

Some animals _____ for food.

4   grind   bite

Pointed teeth can _____.

5   Omnivores   Herbivores

_____ eat meat and plants.

I Write About It

1 Use the words in the word bank to complete each sentence.

Word Bank

meat   plants   meat and plants

A raccoon likes to eat _____.

A deer likes to eat _____.

A wolf likes to eat _____.

2 Can a raccoon and a deer eat the same kind of food?
Write about it.

_____

_____

_____

_____

_____

_____

I Read and Understand

Read the sentence. Mark the best answer.

1 Goats and deer like to eat ____.

○ bugs

○ plants

○ meat

2 A carnivore has teeth that are ____.

○ pointed

○ flat

○ soft

3 An omnivore has ____ teeth.

○ all flat

○ all pointed

○ flat and pointed

4 *Goats* and *Wild About Food* are mostly about ____.

○ animal teeth and food

○ an animal herd

○ how animals hunt

I Can!

> I can tell about the teeth of herbivores, carnivores, and omnivores. I can tell about what they eat.

1 Draw a picture of each kind of teeth.

herbivore	carnivore	omnivore

2 Write a sentence that tells why a bear needs sharp and flat teeth.

_____

_____

_____

3 Write a sentence that tells why a tiger can't mow grass for you.

_____

_____

_____

My Country 'Tis of Thee

Name: _____

We sing about
our country.

1

Sweet land of liberty,

We sing about our freedom.

2

Of thee I sing;

We sing about America.

3

Land where my fathers died,

We sing about
our ancestors.

4

Land of the pilgrims' pride,

We sing about
all the people who
came to America.

Statue
of Liberty

5

We sing about
our beautiful land.

6

We sing about
living with freedom.

We ring the bell
for America!

Liberty Bell

7

Dictionary

Read each word aloud.

America

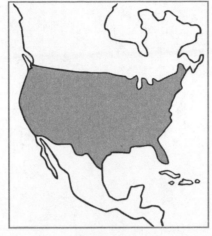

country

Liberty Bell

pilgrims

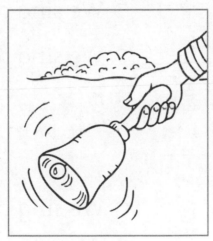

ring

Statue of Liberty

Words to Know

| about | ancestors | beautiful | freedom |
| land | living | people | sing |

I Read Closely

Look at the picture. Read the sentences.
Mark the sentence that goes with the picture.

1

○ We sing about our ancestors.

○ We sing about the land.

2

○ We sing about the bell.

○ We sing about our freedom.

3

○ We sing about the land.

○ We sing about people.

4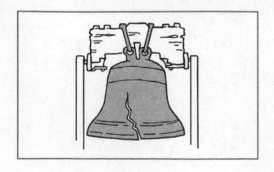

○ We sing about our country.

○ We ring the bell for America.

I Use New Words

Write the missing word to complete the sentence.
Then read the sentence.

1   freedom   living

"Liberty" means _____.

2   ring   sing

We can _____ about our country.

3   Statue of Liberty   America

The Liberty Bell is a symbol for _____.

4   ancestors   country

We are living after our _____.

5   land   pilgrims

The _____ went to a new country to live.

I Write About It

1 Draw a picture of something that you like to do in America.
Then write about it.

_____

_____

_____

_____

_____

_____

2 Draw a picture of something that will make America better for people.
Then write about it.

_____

_____

_____

_____

_____

_____

Reading Paired Text • EMC 6421 • © Evan-Moor Corp.

A Flag for America

Name: _____

Long ago, people came to America.
They lived in colonies.
Some colonies had flags.

1

The colonies had leaders.
One of them was George Washington.
They wanted a new flag.

2

In 1776, George Washington asked
Betsy Ross to sew the new flag.

The leaders liked the new flag. It had
one star and one stripe for each colony.
There were 13 colonies.

4

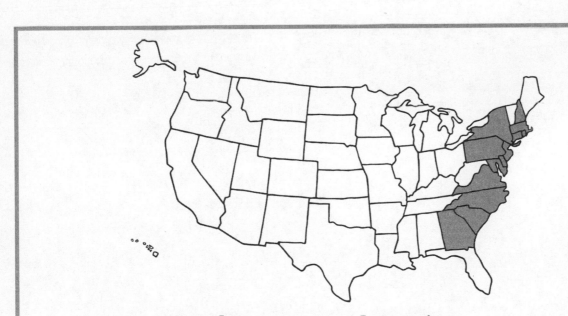

More people came to America.
The colonies became states.
The flag got a star for each new state.

5

Now America has 50 states.
The flag has 50 stars for 50 states.
The flag still has 13 stripes.

6

We see the flag in a lot of places.
It is a symbol for America.

7

Dictionary

Read each word aloud.

America

Betsy Ross

colonies

George
Washington

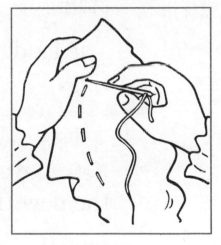

sew

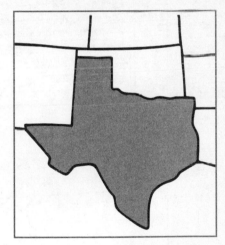

state

Words to Know

asked	flag	leaders	lived
more	people	places	star
stripe	symbol		

I Read Closely

Look at the picture. Read the sentences.
Mark the sentence that goes with the picture.

1

○ People lived in colonies.

○ People lived in states.

2

○ The leaders wanted a new state.

○ The leaders wanted a new flag.

3

○ Betsy Ross was asked to sew the new flag.

○ People see the flag in a lot of places.

4

○ Now the flag has 50 stars.

○ Now the flag has 80 stars.

I Use New Words

Write the missing word to complete the sentence.
Then read the sentence.

1 Betsy Ross   George Washington

_____ could sew well.

2 Leaders   Colonies

_____ are where people lived.

3 people   states

America has 50 _____.

4 Betsy Ross   George Washington

_____ was a leader.

5 symbol   star

The flag is a _____ for America.

I Write About It

1   How did George Washington help get a new flag? Write about it.

_____

_____

_____

_____

_____

2   How did Betsy Ross help make a new flag? Write about it.

_____

_____

_____

_____

_____

I Read and Understand

Read the sentence. Mark the best answer.

1 *My Country 'Tis of Thee* is mostly about _____.

○ how to be a pilgrim

○ a song about freedom

○ a song about a bell

2 *A Flag for America* is mostly about _____.

○ living in colonies

○ Betsy Ross

○ a new flag

3 Songs and symbols help us think about _____.

○ ancestors and freedom

○ people living in a state

○ places with new flags

4 Today, the American flag has _____.

○ 50 stars and 50 stripes

○ 13 stars and 13 stripes

○ 50 stars and 13 stripes

I Can!

> I can write about a song and a symbol of America.

1 Color the first American flag.

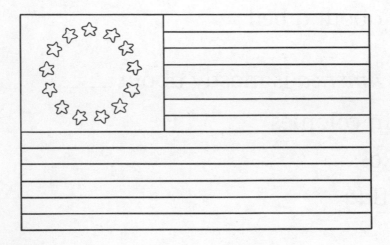

2 Write about a song and a symbol of America.
What do they mean to you?

_____

_____

_____

_____

_____

_____

Big Question
What do you think when you look at art?

The Wonder of Art

Name: _____

People who make art are called artists.
Artists can be young or old.

1

Artists look at the world around them.
They paint or draw or make something.

2

Art can make people feel happy.
Art can make people feel sad.
Art can make people wonder.

3

One artist really made people wonder.
He lived 500 years ago.
His name was Leonardo da Vinci.

4

People still wonder about his famous
painting called the *Mona Lisa*.

5

They wonder why she has a little smile.
They wonder what she is thinking about.

6

Art can be fun.
It can show how you feel.
It can show what you think.
It can show how you see the world.

7

Dictionary

Read each word aloud.

art

artist

draw

paint

painting

world

Words to Know

around	called	famous	feel
old	show	something	still
thinking	wonder	years	young

I Read Closely

Look at the picture. Read the sentences.
Mark the sentence that goes with the picture.

○ Artists paint or draw or make something.

○ Artists run and jump.

○ Art can make people feel hot or cold.

○ Art can make people feel happy or sad.

○ Leonardo da Vinci lived 500 years ago.

○ Leonardo da Vinci lived 100 years ago.

○ People wonder why Mona Lisa looks sad.

○ People wonder why Mona Lisa has a little smile.

I Use New Words

Write the missing word to complete the sentence.
Then read the sentence.

1   artists   paintings

People who make art are _____.

2   think   smile

When I feel happy, I _____.

3   world   famous

The *Mona Lisa* is a _____ painting.

4   young   old

A child is _____.

5   show   wonder

Art can _____ how you feel.

I Write About It

1 See the *Mona Lisa* painting. Look at her eyes and her smile.
Draw a picture of yourself in the box next to her.

2 Write to tell what you are thinking about.

_____

_____

_____

_____

_____

_____

Big Question
What do you think when you look at art?

A Day in the Country

Name: _____

I'm Sofia, and this is my dog Gus.
Today we are going to the country!

1

We put a lot of things into the car.
We are ready to go!

2

We drive and drive.
I draw a picture of Gus and me.
We feel excited to go to the country.

3

At last, we get to the country!
We set up our picnic.
We see hills, trees, and a pond.

4

I am too happy to eat.
Gus and I play ball.
We run and play a lot.

5

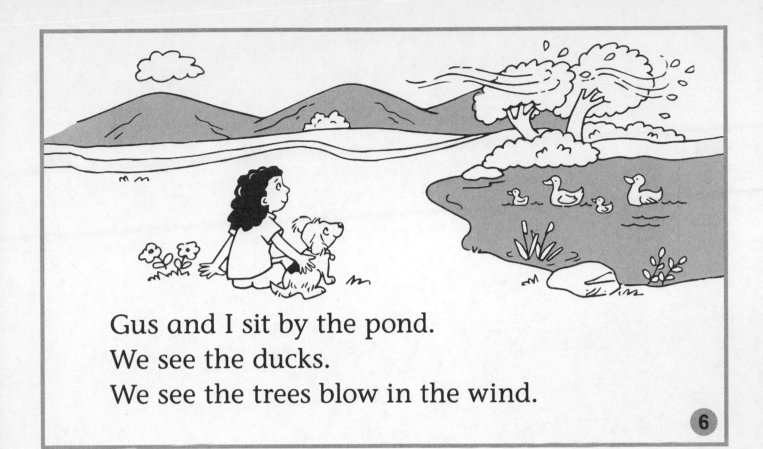

Gus and I sit by the pond.
We see the ducks.
We see the trees blow in the wind.

6

It is time to go.
I will draw a picture of our day.
It will show what we did.
I will remember how we felt.

7

Dictionary

Read each word aloud.

country

draw

hills

picnic

pond

wind

Words to Know

blow	drive	excited	felt
picture	remember	today	

I Read Closely

Look at the picture. Read the sentences.
Mark the sentence that goes with the picture.

 1

○ We drive and drive.

○ We set up our picnic.

2

○ I eat a lot.

○ Gus and I play ball.

3

○ Gus and I sit by the trees.

○ Gus and I sit by the pond.

4

○ I draw a picture to remember our day.

○ We see the trees blow in the wind.

I Use New Words

Write the missing word to complete the sentence.
Then read the sentence.

1   remember   drive

My mom can _____ the car.

2   wind   country

Trees blow in the _____.

3   pond   hills

We are going up and down the _____.

4   draw   drive

You can _____ a picture.

5   picnic   today

We ate a lot of food at our _____.

I Write About It

1   Draw a picture of Sofia doing something that made her feel happy.

2   Write a sentence that tells about your picture.

_____

_____

_____

3   Why does Sofia like to draw pictures? Write a sentence that tells about it.

_____

_____

_____

I Read and Understand

Read the sentence. Mark the best answer.

1 An artist _____.

○ can't feel happy or sad

○ can be young, but not old

○ draws, paints, or makes something

2 Leonardo da Vinci _____.

○ painted the *Mona Lisa*

○ had a dog named Gus

○ lived ten years ago

3 People wonder why Mona Lisa has a little _____.

○ cat

○ smile

○ family

4 Who tells the story in *A Day in the Country*?

○ Gus

○ Sofia

○ Leonardo da Vinci

I Can!

> I can show how art has meaning to the artist and to the people who see it.

1 Draw a picture of a friend.
Then write a sentence that tells about the friend.

_____

_____

_____

_____

2 Draw a picture that shows you having a fun day.
Then write a sentence that tells about it.

_____

_____

Ideas and Inventions

Some people have a lot of ideas. They use their ideas to make inventions. Inventions can help people.

Catherine Wong

Catherine Wong was 17 years old. She saw that many people need a heart doctor. Some doctors are far away. Catherine had an idea. Most people have a cellphone. She invented a way to do a heartbeat test on a cellphone. The test can be sent to the doctor. Then the doctor looks at it. It shows if your heartbeat is good. Catherine's invention will help people.

Daniel Chao was 10 years old. He had reading homework every day. He had to write on a calendar how many minutes he read. Every month he had to take it to his teacher. Daniel wanted to think of an easier way.

Then he had an idea. Daniel invented a calendar app. Students enter the minutes they read on the calendar. Then they send the calendar to their teacher's computer. The app made it easier for students to track their reading every month!

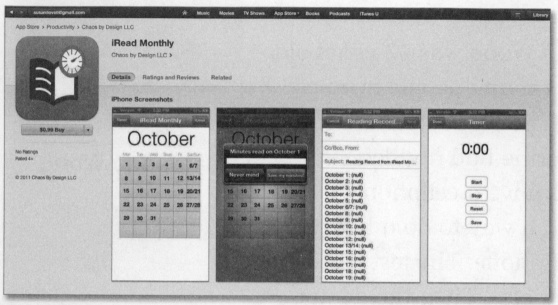

Daniel Chao's app

Catherine and Daniel had good ideas. They made their ideas into inventions. Their inventions help people.

Dictionary

Read each word aloud.

calendar

cellphone

computer

doctor

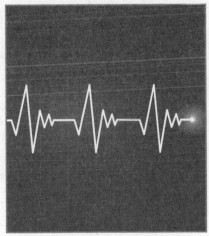

heartbeat test

teacher

Words to Know

app	easier	enter	far
heart	homework	idea	invention
minutes	month	reading	students
track	years		

I Read Closely

Look at the picture. Read the sentences.
Mark the sentence that goes with the picture.

1

   ○ Catherine Wong was 17 years old.

   ○ Catherine Wong was 27 years old.

2

   ○ Most people have a cellphone.

   ○ Most people have a test.

3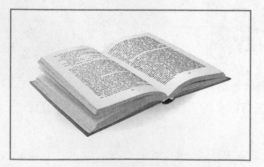

   ○ Daniel Chao had to write down how many minutes he read.

   ○ Daniel Chao did not have to do reading homework.

4

   ○ A lot of students use a cellphone.

   ○ A lot of students use a computer.

I Use New Words

Write the missing word to complete the sentence.
Then read the sentence.

1   idea   app

You need an _____ to make an invention.

2   month   homework

Do your _____ after school.

3   heartbeat   track

A doctor wants to see a _____ test.

4   teacher   heart

Your _____ needs to see your homework.

5   student   computer

An app works on a _____.

I Write About It

1 Draw a picture of the invention that helps people stay well.
Write a sentence about it.

_____

_____

_____

_____

_____

_____

2 Draw a picture of the invention that helps students do homework.
Write a sentence about it.

_____

_____

_____

_____

_____

_____

Ben Franklin

Ben Franklin was born in 1706.
He liked to read.
Ben had a lot of ideas.

Ben wanted to help people.
People needed light and heat.
People didn't have electricity.

Ben wanted to know about lightning.
He wanted to find out if lightning
was electricity.

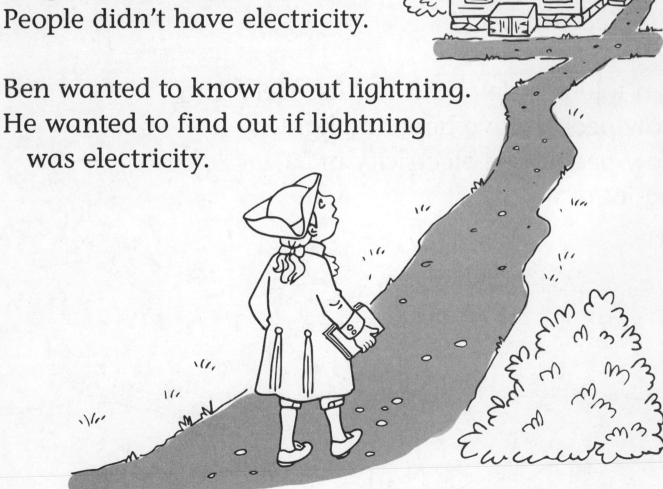

In 1752, Ben made a kite.
He put a key on the kite string.
The rain and lightning came.
He let the kite go up.
He tied the kite string to the ground.

Electricity went down the wet
   kite string.
Ben saw sparks on the key.
Then he knew that lightning
   is electricity.

Ben told people about his discovery.
Now people have heat and light.
Now people use electricity in
   a lot of ways.

Dictionary

Read each word aloud.

Ben Franklin

kite

lightning

sparks

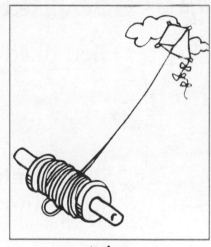

string

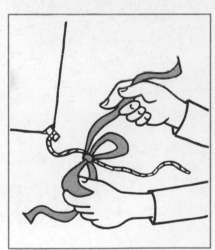

tied

Words to Know

born	discovery	electricity	ground
heat	ideas	knew	light
needed	people	rain	read

I Read Closely

Look at the picture. Read the sentences.
Mark the sentence that goes with the picture.

1

○ Ben Franklin was born in 1706.

○ Ben Franklin was born in 1906.

2

○ Ben liked to play.

○ Ben liked to read.

3

○ Ben wanted to find out if lightning was electricity.

○ Ben wanted to find out if lightning was rain.

4

○ In 1752, Ben made a kite.

○ In 1752, Ben made a string.

I Use New Words

Write the missing word to complete the sentence.
Then read the sentence.

1   electricity   discovery

We use _____ for light and heat.

2   heat   ground

I walk on the _____.

3   string   rain

A kite has a _____ tied to it.

4   ideas   lightning

Out in the rain, we saw _____.

5   kite   knew

You can fly a _____.

I Write About It

1   Draw a picture of Ben's discovery.

2   Write about Ben's discovery.

_____

_____

_____

_____

_____

Word Bank

electricity   lightning   rain   sparks

I Read and Understand

Read the sentence. Mark the best answer.

1 Ben Franklin discovered _____.

○ electricity

○ a computer

○ a cellphone

2 Catherine Wong made _____ to do on a cellphone.

○ a kite

○ homework

○ a heartbeat test

3 Daniel Chao's invention helps keep track of _____.

○ heartbeat tests

○ reading minutes

○ ways people use electricity

4 Catherine Wong, Daniel Chao, and Ben Franklin _____.

○ had ideas to make our lives better

○ had a great way to make a kite

○ gave up on their ideas

I Can!

> I can tell how an idea helped people make an invention or discovery.

Think about what you read. Write about Catherine Wong, Daniel Chao, and Ben Franklin. Tell how their ideas helped them make an invention or discovery.

_____

_____

_____

_____

_____

_____

_____

_____

Word Bank

app	doctor	electricity
heartbeat test	kite	lightning
minutes	reading homework	teacher